COULD A WALRUS PLAY THE SAXOPHONE?

And Other Questions About Animals

Paul Mason

Raintree

Chicago, Illinois

Edited by Dan Nunn, Rebecca Rissman,
  and John-Paul Wilkins
Designed by Steve Mead
Picture research by Mica Brancic
Production by Sophia Argyris
Originated by Capstone Global Library Ltd

Library of Congress Cataloging-in-Publication Data
Cataloging-in-Publication data is available at the
Library of Congress: loc.gov

ISBN 978-1-4109-5197-7 (hardback)
ISBN 978-1-4109-5203-5 (paperback)

Acknowledgments
We would like to thank the following for permission
to reproduce photographs: Getty Images pp. 7
(Gallo Images/Federico Veronesi), 9 (Flickr/© 2006
Sean McCann), 23 (Peter Arnold/Jeffrey L. Rotman);
Science Photo Library p. 21 (Visuals Unlimited, Inc./
Eric Tourneret); Shutterstock pp. 4 orchestra (©
Ferenc Szelepcsenyi), 4 walrus (© ericlefrancais), 4
saxophone (© kuznetcov_konstantin), 5 walrus (© yui),
5 saxophone (© kuznetcov_konstantin), 6 (© jorisvo),
8 earwig (© Scott Hussey), 8 lady's ear (© Tatjana
Romanova), 10 man in swimming gear (© Lilyana
Vynogradova), 10 water background (© Clover), 10
medusa (© Jiri Vaclavek), 11 man in swimming gear (©
Lilyana Vynogradova), 11 toilet (© Jiri Hera), 11 plastic
bucket (© Andrey Eremin), 12 cow (© Dudarev Mikhail),
12 bomb explosion (© James Thew), 13 (© majeczka),
14 (© wtamas), 15 earthworm (© D. Kucharski & K.
Kucharska), 15 soil background (© PhotoHouse), 16
detective with magnifying glass (© Richard Peterson),
16 green plastic plate with crumbs (© Jaimie Duplass),
16 bloodhound dog (© Susan Schmitz), 16 wooden
table (© MaxPhotographer), 17 (© Jostein Hauge), 18
witch (© Fer Gregory), 18 toad (© alexsvirid), 19 toad (©
Angelo Giampiccolo), 19 male hand (© hans.slegers),
20 cow (© arniep), 20 map (© Atlaspix), 20 weather
symbols (© mesimply), 22 lemon shark (© FAUP), 22
hypnotic whirlpool eye (© Biczó Zsolt), 22 silver pocket
watch (© Graça Victoria), 22 water background (©
Clover), 24 (© Daniel Alvarez), 25 (© Bridgena Barnard),
26 (© Matej Kastelic), 27 red sports car (© Charlie
Hutton), 27 skittles (© Becky Stares), 27 bull (© Vera
Zinkova), 27 coloured footballs (© Perry Correll), 28
goldfish (© dibrova), 28 gameshow host (© criben), 29
(© Richard Peterson).

Cover photographs of walrus (© Nejron Photo) and
saxophone (© kuznetcov_konstantin) reproduced with
permission of Shutterstock.

We would like to thank Diana Bentley and Marla Conn
for their invaluable help in the preparation of this book.

Every effort has been made to contact copyright
holders of any material reproduced in this book. Any
omissions will be rectified in subsequent printings if
notice is given to the publisher.

Disclaimer
All the Internet addresses (URLs) given in this book were
valid at the time of going to press. However, due to
the dynamic nature of the Internet, some addresses
may have changed, or sites may have changed or
ceased to exist since publication. While the author and
publisher regret any inconvenience this may cause
readers, no responsibility for any such changes can be
accepted by either the author or the publisher.

Printed in the United States   5483

CONTENTS

Some words are shown in bold, **like this.** You can find out what they mean by looking in the glossary.

COULD A WALRUS PLAY THE SAXOPHONE?

If you visited the zoo in Istanbul, Turkey, you might think the answer was "yes." Sara the walrus appears with her saxophone and puts it in her mouth. The music quickly starts.

Sadly, walruses are not equipped to play the saxophone in real life. Sara is just **miming**. The music actually comes from a sound system!

Big flippers + tiny buttons = impossible to play notes!

WHAT ARE CROCODILE TEARS?

Crocodiles do not cry because they are sad! The crying actually happens when they eat. This is because crocodiles cannot chew. They have to swallow their food in big chunks. Gulping down these chunks forces **fluid** from **glands** around their eyes.

BOO HOO!

A crocodile's tears are difficult to spot because they are always soaking wet!

COULD AN EARWIG CRAWL INTO YOUR EAR?

Even medical books used to say that earwigs sometimes crawled into people's ears. Earwigs do like warm, moist places. Fortunately, though, these places do *not* include human ears!

Did you know?
Although they have wings, earwigs hardly ever fly.

Earwigs were named because of the shape of their wings. When stretched out, they look like human ears.

CAN YOU CURE A JELLYFISH STING BY PEEING ON IT?

Jellyfish stings happen when a jellyfish leaves tiny stingers in your skin. These contain **venom**. Washing jellyfish stings with pee is said to **cure** them. In fact, it will probably make the stingers release *extra* venom. Ow!

Some experts say the best way to treat most jellyfish stings is to wash them with saltwater.

saltwater

pee

COULD COWS REALLY DESTROY THE WORLD?

Have cows developed a super-bomb to blow us all up? No! It is cow farts that some people worry about. These people think that cow farts contain gases that cause **global warming** to get worse.

moooo!

This is wrong, of course. It is cow burps, not farts, that could destroy the world!

cow fart does little harm

cow burp contains gas that is terrible for the environment

DOES CUTTING A WORM IN HALF MAKE TWO WORMS?

No. If you accidentally cut an earthworm in two, the best result would be:

- one shorter worm
- one dead piece of worm.

A worm can only survive being cut in two if it happens near its tail. If you cut it in the middle, both parts would wriggle as if they were alive. Then they would die.

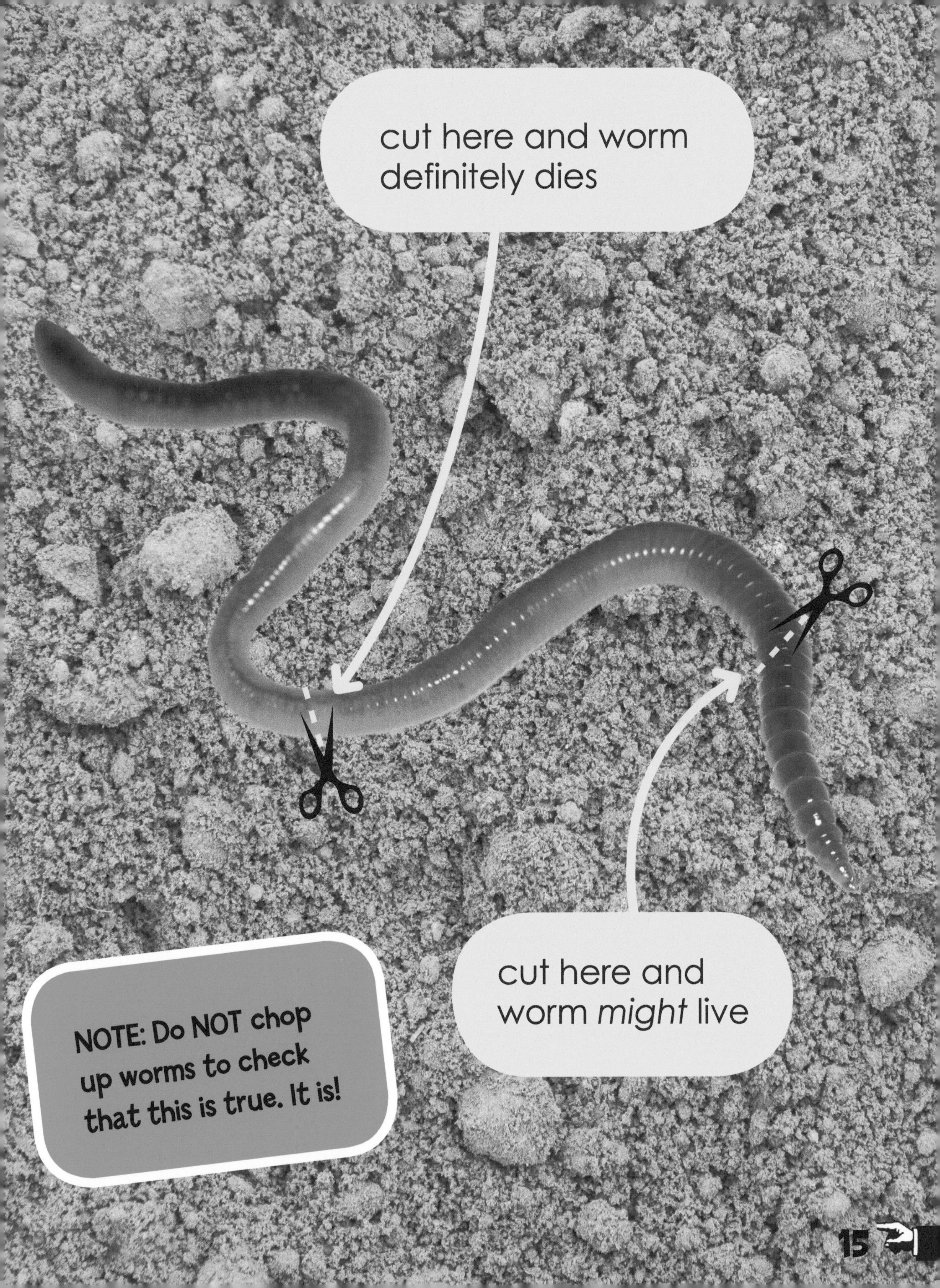

NOTE: Do NOT chop up worms to check that this is true. It is!

DO DOGS LEAVE FINGERPRINTS?

No—but if you think Fido's been stealing your cookies, there might be another way to find out. Each dog's nose print is as **unique** as a human fingerprint.

"It wasn't me... honest!"

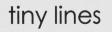

tiny lines

shape of
nostrils

Did you know?
Up to a third of a dog's brain
may be used for smells!

CAN YOU CATCH WARTS FROM A TOAD?

Toads do *look* warty. It is no wonder people used to think they could catch **warts** from them. In fact, the lumps and bumps on a toad's skin are not warts. They are **glands**. When a toad is scared, the glands release a slimy liquid called mucus. Some toads even release poison!

CAN COWS FORECAST THE WEATHER?

Some people claim that cows lie down when they sense rain is coming. This is not true, though. Cows actually lie down after eating food.

And now for the weather...

Did you know?

Some animals do seem to be able to **predict** storms:
- Sharks head for deep water.
- Birds go to their nests.
- Bees take shelter in their **hives**.

CAN YOU HYPNOTIZE A SHARK?

Sharks are feared around the world. But some sharks can be **hypnotized**—just by rubbing the tip of their nose! Even deadly killers such as the great white shark can be affected.

How to hypnotize a shark

Step 1. Rub shark's nose
Step 2. Stand shark on head
Step 3. Rub nose more.

The shark will be hypnotized for 15 minutes!

23

DO HYENAS REALLY LAUGH?

Hyenas crunch through bone with their powerful jaws. They can run faster than a human. They are so nasty that people even say hyenas laugh when they kill something. This is not actually true, though. The noise *sounds* like laughter to us. But it is just one hyena telling another that it can eat first.

Ha! Ha!

25

DOES RED REALLY MAKE BULLS ANGRY?

There is an old saying that something that makes you angry is "like a red flag to a bull." In fact, bulls may not even see red. They are likely to confuse it with blue or green.

Is the red **cape** making this bull angry—or is the man sticking hooks into him the problem?

Actually, they all look green to me. Or is it blue?

DO GOLDFISH REALLY HAVE BAD MEMORIES?

Goldfish are said to have three-second memories. In fact, they are quite good at remembering things. Goldfish have been taught to fetch objects and other tricks. They even remember the tricks months later.

What is the capital of France?

Umm...

Did you know?

Elephants have great memories. They can recognize old friends from years ago.

GLOSSARY

cape sleeveless coat that is tied around the neck and hangs down around a person's body

cure make someone who is unwell better

fluid liquid without a fixed shape, such as water

gland part of an animal that releases liquid

global warming increase in Earth's temperature. Global warming is responsible for changes in our weather and more natural disasters.

hive place where bees live

hypnotize put into a dreamy state of mind, in which you do not act for yourself

miming pretending you are doing something, but without actually doing it

predict say what will happen in the future

unique one of a kind

venom substance that is harmful when injected under the skin

wart small, hard lump on the skin

FIND OUT MORE

Books

Dorling Kindersley Animal Encyclopedia. New York: Dorling Kindersley, 2000.

Ganeri, Anita. *Animal Top Tens series.* Chicago: Raintree, 2008.

Seuling, Barbara. *Cows Sweat Through Their Noses: And Other Freaky Facts About Animal Habits, Characteristics, and Homes.* Minneapolis: Picture Window, 2008.

Wild Animal Atlas: Earth's Astonishing Animals and Where They Live. Washington, D.C.: National Geographic Kids, 2010.

Web sites

Facthound offers a safe, fun way to find Internet sites related to this book. All of the sites on Facthound have been researched by our staff.

Here's all you do:
Visit www.facthound.com
Type in this code: 9781410951977

INDEX

Questions You Never Thought You'd Ask

COULD A WALRUS PLAY THE SAXOPHONE?

And other questions about Animals

- Could a walrus play the saxophone?
- Could an earwig crawl into your ear?
- Can cows forecast the weather?

This book takes a fun look at animals by asking and answering a series of quirky yet thought-provoking questions. Although primarily a recreational read, the book contains a wealth of fascinating information and bizarre facts about animals that readers will be sure to find captivating.

Titles in the **Questions You Never Thought You'd Ask** series:
Can You Lick Your Own Elbow?
Could a Robot Make My Dinner?
Could a Walrus Play the Saxophone?
Could I Sit on a Cloud?
Did the Romans Eat Chips?

This **Read Me!** series delivers high-interest, curriculum-relevant topics at an accessible reading level, through exciting visual design and simple text. Use **Read Me!** books to interest reluctant readers, extend a course of study, or just for fun!

About the Author
Paul Mason has spent his life finding out useless information. Is it possible to be sucked down an airplane toilet? Should you suck the venom from a snake bite? It has all been perfect training for writing a book like this one!

Level O

ISBN 978-1-4109-5203-5

a capstone imprint   www.capstonepub.com

9 781410 952035
90000